PENGUINS

SEYMOUR SIMON

Smithsonian | Collins

An Imprint of HarperCollinsPublishers

Emperor penguin chicks

Special thanks to Gary Graves, Curator, National Museum of Natural History, Smithsonian Institution, for his invaluable contribution to this book.

PHOTO CREDITS: Pages 2, 22: Tim Davis / Photo Researchers, Inc.; pages 3, 8, 21, 26: Rod Planck / Dembinsky Photo Associates; pages 4–5: M. P. Kahl / Photo Researchers, Inc.; page 7: Daniel A. Bedell / AnimalsAnimals; page 9: © Tui De Roy / Minden Pictures; pages 10, 17: Johnny Johnson / AnimalsAnimals; page 13: James Brandt / AnimalsAnimals; pages 14–15: © Steve Bloom / stevebloom.com; pages 18–19, 25: Fritz Polking / Dembinsky Photo Associates; page 29: Marian Bacon / AnimalsAnimals; page 30: Mark J. Thomas / Dembinsky Photo Associates.

The name of the Smithsonian, Smithsonian Institution and the sunburst logo
are registered trademarks of the Smithsonian Institution.
Collins is an imprint of HarperCollins Publishers.

Library of Congress Cataloging-in-Publication Data
Simon, Seymour.
  Penguins / Seymour Simon.— 1st ed.
    p.   cm.— (Smithsonian)
  ISBN 978-0-06-028395-7 (trade bdg.) — ISBN 978-0-06-028396-4 (lib. bdg.) — ISBN 978-0-06-446221-1 (pbk.)
  1. Penguins—Juvenile literature. I. Title. II. Series.
QL696.S473S546 2007   2006024116
598.47—dc22   CIP
                                                                              AC

14 15 16 SCP 10 9 8 7 6 5
❖
First Edition

Adélie penguins

To my son, Michael Simon, former president
of the Penguin Club (in elementary school)

Smithsonian Mission Statement

For more than 160 years, the Smithsonian has remained true to its mission, "the increase and diffusion of knowledge." Today the Smithsonian is not only the world's largest provider of museum experiences supported by authoritative scholarship in science, history, and the arts but also an international leader in scientific research and exploration. The Smithsonian offers the world a picture of America, and America a picture of the world.

Penguins are champion swimmers and divers. But they are not fish and they are not aquatic mammals such as dolphins. Penguins are birds because they have feathers, and only birds have feathers. Like birds, they lay their eggs and raise their chicks on land. But they don't look or fly like most other birds. Instead, they seem to fly through the water, and they spend much of their lives at sea.

All penguins live in the Southern Hemisphere, from frozen Antarctica to the warmer waters of the Galápagos Islands near the equator. Penguins are defenseless, so they usually live in out-of-the-way places, safe from most enemies.

Since penguins are very social, their nesting areas, called rookeries, may contain thousands of pairs of birds crowded up against one another, such as these king penguins. Even at sea, penguins usually swim and feed in groups. The penguin colonies on Antarctica are huge, containing twenty million or more penguins at times during the year.

Penguins have big heads and short, thick necks. Some penguins have crests and differently colored heads and bills. Black, blue, or gray feathers usually cover the upper parts of their bodies. Their legs are set low on their bodies, and they waddle from side to side as they walk. If people waddled like penguins, they would fall over easily. But penguins rarely seem to trip and fall down.

The seventeen penguin species live in many different places, but all penguins feed at sea like this emperor penguin. Some dive as deep as 1,500 feet to find food. Their main meals are small fish and squid. Antarctic penguins also feed on krill.

A penguin's tongue and throat have stiff, backward-facing barbs that help grip slippery food and keep it from sliding out. When a penguin swallows food underwater, it also ingests salt water. Special glands drain the salt water into the penguin's nose. The salt water runs off its nose when the penguin surfaces.

Paddlelike flippers, a short, wedge-shaped tail, and webbed feet help make penguins good swimmers. Some penguins spend three-quarters of their lives in the water, occasionally for months at a time. Penguins have a streamlined body shape in the water. A mid-sized penguin can slice through the water like an arrow cutting through the air. The penguin hunches its head into its shoulders and presses its feet close to its body against its tail to help steer.

In the water, the motion of a penguin's flippers resembles the wing movements of birds in flight. Their heavy, solid bones help penguins

Adélie penguins

King penguins

stay underwater and keep them from bobbing to the surface. Penguin eyes are large and help them see clearly underwater as well as on land. Penguins can stay underwater for ten to fifteen minutes before coming to the surface to breathe.

Most penguins can swim five or six miles per hour. However, some can put on a blazing burst of speed of as much as fifteen miles per hour. The fastest a person has ever run in one hour is a little over thirteen miles.

Even though penguins spend much of their lives at sea, they all return to land to lay eggs. The season for mating depends upon the penguin species and habitat. In temperate zones, breeding season is often in the spring. During the mating season, penguins head for a rookery.

When he is ready to mate, the male stands, arches his back, and stretches out his flippers. He makes loud calls and waves his head and flippers. He bows, struts about, and may offer a rock as a gift. If fights break out, the males use their bills and flippers to hit their rivals.

When penguins, like the king penguins on the left, find their mates, they bond by touching necks and slapping each other on the back with their flippers. By "singing" to each other, they learn to recognize each other's voice. A penguin may stay with its mate for years—or as long as the pair has chicks together.

In about four days, most kinds of penguins lay two eggs. Both parents take turns sitting on the eggs for about four or more weeks, depending on the species of penguin. During incubation, the brood patch, an area of skin on the lower abdomen, becomes swollen and warm.

The chick uses its egg tooth (a small point on the tip of the bill) to break through the eggshell. Within a few weeks, the chick grows feathers that provide insulation against the cold. While their parents search for food at sea, chicks often stay in groups called crèches for safety and warmth.

Adélie penguins

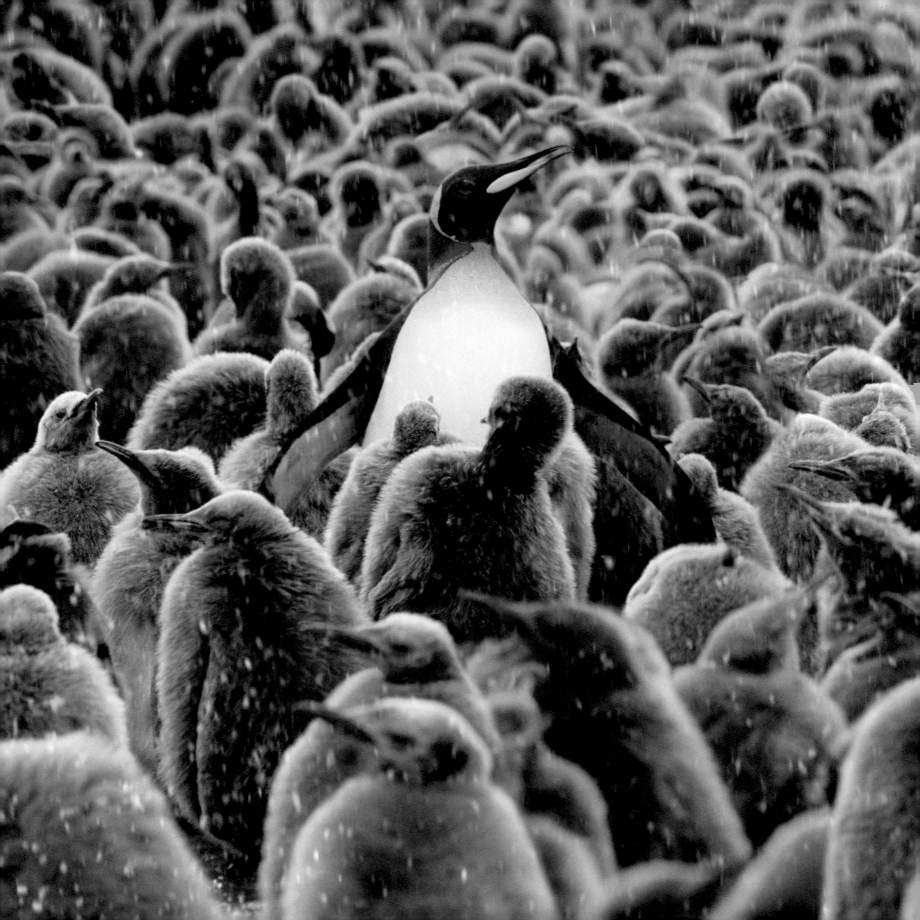

Chicks beg for food from any passing adult or even other chicks. So adults identify their own chicks, like these king penguin chicks, by recognizing their distinctive calls. When a chick pecks around a parent's bill, the parent feeds it partially digested food from the parent's stomach.

When chicks are ready to leave the nest, they shed their first feathers and develop waterproof feathers. Now they are fledglings. Before long, they will make their first journey to the sea to build up their body fat.

Besides the lack of food and bad weather, penguin chicks have to contend with many dangers, particularly from predators such as mustelids, rats, dogs, pigs, gulls, sheathbills, and giant petrels. But the skua, an Antarctic seabird, is a chick's worst enemy. While in flight, a skua can pick up and swallow a small chick in a single gulp. On the ground, a powerful skua can catch and drag a good-sized chick away from the protection of the colony.

Adult penguins have no natural enemies on land, but at sea they are preyed upon by leopard seals, killer whales, fur seals, sea lions, and sharks. A leopard seal (right) swims along the edges of the ice pack or hides under ice floes waiting for penguins to dive into the water.

Emperors, the largest penguins in the world, stand up to four feet high and weigh as much as a hundred pounds. The emperors spend cold, windy winters on the open Antarctic ice, a hundred or more miles inland.

To stay warm, emperors clump together in huge, huddled masses. They take turns moving to the inside of the group, where they're partly protected from the frigid winds that howl at more than a hundred miles per hour along the ice.

After a courtship of several weeks, a female emperor lays a single egg and leaves it atop the feet of her mate. She immediately departs for the distant sea to feed. For about sixty-five days through blinding storms and, sometimes, below-freezing temperatures, the father balances the egg on his feet and keeps it warm by covering it with his brood patch.

Finally, the mothers return at the time the chicks are hatching. They take over the feedings, and the males head to sea. Seven or eight weeks later, the chicks are large enough to make their trip.

King penguins are second in size only to emperors. A king is almost three feet tall and can weigh nearly thirty-five pounds. It lives on the cold, rocky coasts of islands surrounding Antarctica. The king penguin has golden-orange swatches on its neck and around its head, a white belly, and a blue-black back. Kings don't waddle the way most penguins do. Instead, they run fairly quickly on their feet.

Nesting colonies of up to ten thousand kings form onshore. Each penguin keeps its neighbor at an exact but close distance away. If a neighbor gets too close, it gets a nasty slap from a flipper or a jab from a beak.

King penguin

Gentoo penguins can grow as tall as thirty inches and can weigh up to thirteen pounds. Their colorful orange bill sets them apart from other penguins. Also, no other penguin has such a big tail.

Most gentoos live in large colonies along the coasts of Antarctica. Gentoos stay with their mates throughout the year. Mating pairs usually build nests of pebbles on bare ground. Year after year, they may return to the same inland nest to lay their two eggs.

Macaroni penguins (right) get their name from the long orange, yellow, and black feathery crests that rise above their eyes. They were named after a macaroni dandy, a hairstyle that was fashionable in the eighteenth century. Macaronis stand about twenty-seven inches high and weigh about nine pounds. They live around Antarctica, mostly on South Georgia, Crozet, Kerguelen, and Heard Islands.

Breeding season for macaronis starts in December when mating pairs lay two different-sized eggs. The first egg is half the size of the second egg and usually does not hatch.

Rockhoppers, the smallest of the Antarctic penguins, are slightly taller than twenty inches and weigh only five and a half pounds. They live among the macaronis. Like the macaronis, they have feathered crests on their heads and have similar nesting and breeding habits. But rockhoppers are more aggressive than macaronis.

Adélie penguin

Adélie penguins were named after the wife of Dumont d'Urville, one of the early explorers of the Antarctic. Adélies are small penguins, about twenty-seven inches in height, and weigh about ten or eleven pounds.

Adélies spend the harsh Antarctic winter months near the outer edges of the ice pack, where it is slightly warmer. They often stay at sea, resting in groups on pack ice and icebergs. As summer approaches, they breed on the coast or on barren island beaches. Adélie rookeries range in size from less than one hundred to hundreds of thousands of chicks.

Chinstrap penguins are the same size as Adélies. They get their name from a thin black line that circles under the chin, like a strap on a helmet. They breed in slightly warmer waters on islands off the coast of Antarctica. One of the largest colonies on Deception Island may have up to a million chinstraps. Chinstraps are among the boldest and most aggressive of all penguins.

Other penguin species:

- Royal penguins have yellow-orange and black crests. Royals are found only on rocky Macquarie Island in the Pacific Ocean south of New Zealand. They are the largest of the crested penguins.

- Erect-crested penguins have long, spiky feathers that stand straight up from their heads. They live in the subantarctic regions of southern New Zealand.

- Blue or little or fairy penguins are the smallest of all the penguins. Blues stand sixteen inches high and weigh only two pounds. They live in the warmer waters around Australia, Tasmania, and New Zealand.

- Magellanic penguins, the largest of the warm-weather penguins, live on the stormy and rocky shores of southern Argentina and Chile.

- Yellow-eyed penguins, the third largest penguins, have yellow-orange catlike eyes. They live along the coastal shores of New Zealand and neighboring islands.

Magellanic penguin

Despite the harsh weather, the penguins that live in and around Antarctica, such as these chinstrap penguins, survive in large numbers. But penguins that live in climates that are more temperate are not as fortunate. Some kinds are in danger of becoming extinct.

There are only a few thousand Galápagos penguins left because weather and ocean changes known as El Niño have depleted the numbers of fish that they eat. South of Australia, only a few thousand fiordland penguins remain due to the lack of fish.

The development of coasts, overfishing, and pollution have also affected the penguin population. Pollution in ocean waters reduces the ability of penguins to lay eggs that hatch successfully. Some researchers estimate that tens of thousands of penguins are killed each year by oil spills. Along the Australian and New Zealand coasts, cats, dogs, and other animals feed on penguin chicks.

Each penguin species struggles in a different way to survive. By learning more about penguins we can begin to understand how to help them and other endangered sea animals to survive in our changing world.

GLOSSARY

Crèche—A group of young chicks; a nursery. This is where chicks gather for safety when their parents are feeding at sea.

Crest—A ridge of long feathers on a bird's head.

Egg tooth—A raised part of a chick's beak that helps it to hatch; it later falls off.

El Niño—A warm flow of water along the western coast of South America that usually occurs at the same time as heavy amounts of rain.

Fledgling—A young bird that has just grown its adult feathers.

Flipper—A flat limb that is used for swimming and steering.

Incubation—A period of time when the egg is kept at a warm temperature so that the chick inside can grow.

Krill—Very small, shrimplike ocean creatures that are the food source of many ocean animals, including some penguins.

Pack ice—A large area of ice floating on the surface of the ocean.

Rookery—A breeding ground for penguins or other birds.

Southern Hemisphere—The lower half of the earth, south of the equator.

Temperate zone—An area of warm temperatures and moderate climates.

INDEX

READ MORE ABOUT IT

Smithsonian Institution
www.si.edu

Penguin World
www.penguinworld.com

International Penguin Conservation Work Group
www.seabirds.org

OCEANS
by Seymour Simon

PENGUIN CHICK
by Betty Tatham

SHARKS
by Seymour Simon

WHALES
by Seymour Simon